# WAITING FOR LUNCH

# WAITING FOR LUNCH

## Quick, Lively Activities for the Whole Class

By Greta Rasmussen

ISBN 0-936110-02-3
Library of Congress Catalog Card Number: 81-82797


Tin Man Press
Box 219
Stanwood, Wa. 98292

# CONTENTS

# INTRODUCTION

Every teacher knows there are awkward times in the school day when the class is put "on hold" until the next event happens. The most notorious "holding period" is usually just before lunch or at the end of the day, when some classrooms truly turn into "holding pens."

It doesn't need to be that way. Five minutes don't have to seem like an eternity, and you shouldn't have to reach for the aspirin bottle when the children are finally all gone.

In fact, these five minutes can be the best public relations opportunity you have—if you use them to your advantage. Rather that letting students see you at your worst—scolding and scowling—they can see you at your best. And you can share with them in some of the finest moments in the school day.

Fine moments seldom come by accident, however. That is why the activities in this book are carefully structured—it just doesn't show.

Most of the activities which follow should be done orally. In this way ideas can bounce from one student to another and class spirit can grow.

All of the activities here are easy to execute and require practically no teacher preparation. They are designed to be open-ended and interesting to children of varying backgrounds and ability levels.

But there is a price. You the teacher must participate. The activities won't work half as well if you turn them over to your best student to direct while you sit at your desk for five minutes checking papers. If you do that, you are saying, "These activities don't really matter. I have better things to do."

You will find a surprising range of activities in this book—thinking games, pure nonsense, manipulative challenges, sophisticated word play.

The menu is rich and varied. Pick from this smorgasbord with enthusiasm. Make "Waiting for Lunch" an important part of the day.

Greta Rasmussen

# ACTIVITIES

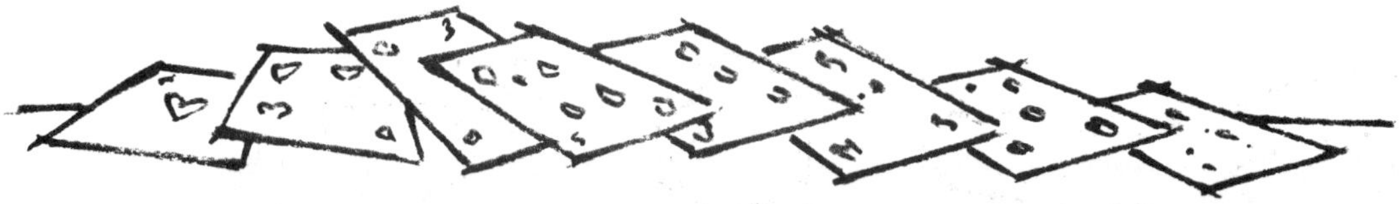

# CARD COMMANDS

Playing cards have all sorts of uses while waiting for lunch. For this activity, remove the face cards, and then give each child a number card, face down.

Next, instruct the class to listen carefully and follow directions, based on the number of the card they are holding. All directions should be done just once, unless otherwise stated.

Fours, stand up and sit down.
Twos, put your hands on your head, then take them off.
Threes, stick out your tongue.
Eights, pretend you are chewing.
Tens, cover up your face.
Ones, smile at the teacher.
Nines, twiddle your thumbs several times.
Sixes, snap your fingers.
Fives, wave.
Tens, look out the window.
Sevens, touch the floor with your left hand.
Ones, slap your own face with your hand.
Twos, walk to the blackboard and back.
Nines, walk around the room once.
Threes, snore.
Eights, shake hands with your neighbor.
Fours, stick your fingers in your ears.
Fives, lean as far as you can to the left.
Sixes, wink twice.
Sevens, pat yourself on the back.

Note: If time permits, re-distribute cards and run through again, as quickly as possible.

# FOOD FOR THOUGHT

Tell the students they are going to be thinking of foods in an entirely new way—by starting with objects that don't have anything to do with food. The shapes of the objects should remind them of certain kinds of foods, however—if they are flexible in their thinking.

Of course, there can be more than one right answer. Here are some possibilities:

Tire—(doughnut)
Icicle—(carrot)
Basketball—(tomato, pea, head lettuce or cabbage, etc.)
Light bulb—(pear)
Frisbee—(pizza)
Umbrella—(mushroom)
Telephone booth—(loaf of bread, candy bar, stick of butter)
Clown's hat—(ice cream cone)
Top—(beet)
Sidewalk—(graham crackers, soda crackers by virtue of segmentation)
Worm—(spaghetti, string beans)
Tree—(celery)
Stop sign—(lollipop)
Rug—(pie dough, cheese slice)

# VITAL STATISTICS

Be the facilitator in the project which follows. Let the students do most of the work. Most will find the mental labor satisfying since it's about them.

You ask the questions.

1. How many people are there in our class?
2. How many fingers in our classroom?
3. How many toes?
4. How many elbows?
5. How many blonds?
6. How many redheads?
7. How many brunettes?
8. How many wear glasses?
9. How many tennis shoes are in the room today?
10. How many people with fillings in their mouths?

# PAPER PLATE SPELLING BEE

Write a letter of the alphabet on each of 26 paper plates. Distribute one plate to each child. If you don't have 26 students, let a couple of children work with two plates, such as an "x" and an "a".

The object is for the children to spell words bodily—by coming to the front of the room with their "letter" and arranging themselves in the proper sequence.

Don't use words which have double letters. The list below should help get you started—every letter in the alphabet is utilized at least once, and the words—(except for the show-off last one) are generally spellable!

storm
zebra
extra
silky
help
wagon

rice
drug
fish
jail
quit
vote
taxidermy

# STRING THE RING!

This activity requires a ball of string and the temporary use of a ring.

Start with the ball of string and give it to the person sitting at the far end of the room. Holding onto the end, he passes the ball to his neighbor, who passes it to his neighbor, and the process continues until every child in the whole room is holding one part of the same line.

Next, the person holding the end of the string (the first person) is given a ring to put on the string.

The object: How fast can the ring move along the string?

Note: Be sure to tell the students to hold onto their part of the string firmly. Yanking is out, naturally. When the ring starts traveling on the string, students will quite rightly want to use the principle of gravity and hold their string at as sharp an angle as possible.

This is a good game to time—to see how fast the ring can be sent around the room.

# HOUSEWORK

Begin the discussion by asking students how many live in houses, how many in apartments. What is an Eskimo house called? A bird's house? A lion's house?

Then ask these questions:

1. If the distance from the floor to the top of your door is seven feet, how far would you guess it was from the floor to your ceiling?

2. What is the main material your outside walls are made of? If wood, what holds the wood together? (nails) What did a carpenter do to put wood together before there were nails? (pegs)

3. How many different walls are there in your house? Count them.

4. How many faucets? Drains?

5. Thinking of your living room floor at home, picture yourself standing on it and think of every single thing which could be under your feet.

6. How many things in your house besides mirrors can you see yourself in? (toaster, spoons, window reflections, etc.)

7. Think of everything in your house that takes electricity.

Note: Discussions are best when they are based on subjects children know well. Talking about their homes, therefore, is a natural.

# WHAT'S HAPPENING?

Ask the children to give their versions of what is going on in these drawings, which you should make one at a time on the board.

You'll notice that the pictures are really very simple. To be successful, such abstractions must not give out too much information. Otherwise, the interpretations are narrow and uninteresting.

The second picture could be a family about ready to go swimming in their pool, trees by a lake, or a brother and sister not wanting to go on a ride in the car with their parents.

The fifth picture might be a computer or a typewriter, or it could be two children who are new on the first day of school.

Each picture should be discussed and then erased, so that students will center on one challenge at a time.

# PAPER PLATE SPIRALS

Children love to make spirals out of paper plates. And they're so easy. Those most talented with the scissors will naturally make the best spirals.

You should demonstrate this activity first. While you are demonstrating, ask children what sprials they see in everyday life. A spiral staircase? A snail? A lady's hairdo?

Tell students to keep their continuous strip as thin as possible in order to produce a long spiral. This is possible since paper plates are made of fairly tough material.

The finished spirals hung in front of the windows or from the ceiling produce some interesting and decorative effects.

# NONSENSE SENTENCES

Children enjoy non sequiturs. They always bring a good laugh. It takes only a few minutes to write the following subjects and predicates on individual note cards. Make the predicates one color, the subjects another, so they don't get mixed up.

Give subject cards to half the class and line them up on one side of the room. The remaining students receive predicate cards and form a line on the other side of the room.

Ask the first subject person and the first predicate person to meet at the center of the room and say their accidental sentences together. When they finish, send them to the back of the line. When the cards run out, simply reshuffle and let the tomfoolery continue.

Don't tell the students they are getting subject and predicate review in the process.

| SUBJECTS | PREDICATES |
|---|---|
| The dog | bit the wall. |
| The kitchen | ate the sink. |
| I | itched a lot |
| Ms. (teacher's name) | lost four teeth. |
| The desk | chewed a worm. |
| An eyelash | gobbled a fly. |
| The little boy's nose | sang a song. |
| The pretty girl's friend | climbed a tree. |
| A poodle | got a black eye. |
| An elbow | kissed a friend. |
| The wall | tickled a grasshopper. |
| His house | smelled like a rotten egg. |
| A baby | coughed up bananas. |
| The queen | blew bubbles. |

# ANOTHER LIST?

List-making is not new to children and it can sometimes be mere busywork. Oral list-making as an activity is included here because the categories call for original thinking.

Each of these categories can make a separate "Waiting for Lunch" session. The process of doing this as a group endeavor, with one idea sparking another, can be an exciting experience.

Ask the children to name everything:

1. Curled
2. With points
3. Invisible
4. That can be popped
5. That costs a quarter
6. That moves in a circle
7. That doesn't make noise
8. That you can peel
9. That is hard to open
10. That has only one moving part

# CLASSROOM CLAIRVOYANCE

(A one-time and one-time-only activity)

This will test your dramatic talents. Announce that you have developed a strange new power. It has come to you overnight. You can now see through the back of your head.

Then ask one student to come to the front of the room. Tell him you're going to turn your back on him while he raises either his right or left hand high over his head and holds it in the air while you count to twenty.

Brag that you are actually watching him through the back of your head while he does this, and after the number twenty is reached, you will turn around and tell him which hand was in the air.

After the count, turn around and face the child. Make a big show of examining his hands and concentrating on the answer very carefully.

The hand which was in the air will be noticeably paler due to the lack of circulation.

Repeat this spectacle with three other children; then confess. Who knows, the frivolous nature of this activity just may lead to an earnest discussion on blood circulation and gravity!

# WORD WANDER

Children love to do this. Call a verbally sophisticated child to the front of the room to be your partner. The object is for the two of you to take turns saying a word until you have completed several sentences to make a story.

Your participation during the first story will help children get the hang of it. Rest assured, you will never get a chance to perform again, since the game is that popular!

For example, you start the story by saying "One." The student will say a word such as "day," and you say "my" and the student says "zipper" and so on.

Naturally, the more action verbs and lively nouns contributed the better! Then choose some other student to take your place for a couple of minutes and keep switching quite often.

This is a good way to learn more about a student's understanding of syntax, by the way.

One word of caution: Always be sure that one of the pair possesses good verbal skills—a strong partner can save even the most limited other member of the duo. Regardless of ability, I've never seen a child who didn't think this was great fun.

Variation: Go around the room, with every student saying a word. This way, everybody plays. An effort must be made to say the words as fast as possible so that the total effect is conversational.

# ACCIDENTAL ART

Give children pieces of flexible string four inches or so long. Have them place drawing paper on their desks and, from a height of two or three feet, drop the string onto the paper.

Ask them to draw a line carefully alongside the string. They are to use the accidental line as the beginning of a drawing of any subject they wish.

Note: It's best to collect the strings once the children have made their accidental lines. There are always a few in every classroom who aren't satisfied with their first "drop" and would do it again and again—getting nothing accomplished but a bunch of squiggles (which, incidentally, would defeat the rationale of the exercise.)

# A DIGITAL DIVERSION

Silence is sometimes golden, especially after a hectic morning. Fingers do the talking in this exercise, where students are told that numbers will be the answers.

Tell them to hold up the appropriate number of fingers for the answers.

Ask children to give you a number that:

| | | |
|---|---|---|
| Rhymes with the place where you can see wild animals | zoo | 2 |
| Sounds the same as the word which means "have eaten" | ate | 8 |
| Rhymes with the thing you usually put a hot dog in | bun | 1 |
| Rhymes with a word you use to describe yourself | me | 3 |
| Rhymes with something you have to go through to get outside | door | 4 |
| Rhymes with the home for something that buzzes | hive | 5 |
| Rhymes with long, skinny things made out of wood | sticks | 6 |
| Rhymes with something you can draw with a pencil | line | 9 |
| Rhymes with something found in the barnyard | hen | 10 |

# MINI-MESSAGES

Legalize note writing by using it as a short, pre-lunch exercise. Make it more interesting by having children write their notes on little two-inch square scraps of paper. Suggest they write as small as possible to see how much they can say!

Have them write the notes to you, and if you're feeling ambitious, tell them you'll answer them.

Also tell them that you're going to give a week of free drinks at the fountain for the person who writes the most!

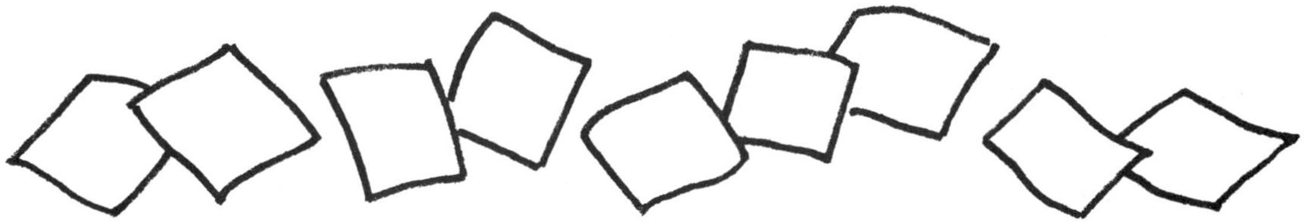

# IN THE BAG

You'll need a lunch sack. After all, this is the "Waiting for Lunch" book. Write the words below on individual slips of paper and put them into the lunch sack.

Have the children pass the sack until you say stop. Whoever is holding the bag, so to speak, has to take out one slip of paper and act out the word written on it.

The sack is then put back into rotation until you say stop again.

It is perhaps best if you don't look at the children while the sack is being passed, so that your stop signal is truly unbiased.

Possible words to use:

Clown
Elephant
Duck
Scarecrow
Dog
Cat
Teacher (you)
Turtle
Horse
Rock star
Mailman
Policeman
Astronaut
Snake
Monkey
Puppet
Lion tamer
Tree
Fish
Rabbit
Barber
Ballet dancer
Baby
Snowman

HELLO

# TALL AND SKINNY

Write the word "Hello" on the board as shown. Be sure to exaggerate the verticality of the letters so that the word is difficult to decipher.

Then ask the children to write a short sentence of their choice using long, skinny writing. Make sure they know the letters are to be not only very long and skinny but written as closely together as possible.

After they have finished their sentences, have them trade papers with their neighbors (or send the papers in a round robin throughout the room!)

Some of the words may be hard to read, but the reading becomes considerably easier when the paper is placed horizontally at eye level. This is due to the principle of foreshortening, and you might introduce the idea in discussion.

# PAPER PLATE PANTOMIME

Each child gets a paper plate for the two activites which follow.

The first assignment involves using the plates in pantomime. Without words, the class must act out each of the ideas you are about to present. The only stipulation is that they must use their paper plates in some imaginative way to carry out the ideas.

Keep your eyes open for a particularly interesting interpretation and have that child repeat his pantomime for the class.

1. You are caught in the rain and you do not want your head to get wet.
2. You have just said something embarrassing and you don't want anyone to see you.
3. "I wish that fly would stop bothering me."
4. A beautiful full moon is coming up.
5. "I think I'll bake a pie."
6. "Oh boy, a pizza!"
7. "I'm really happy."
8. I'm really sad."
9. "Boo-hoo, my balloon broke."
10. "I wonder if this is a snapping turtle."

After the children have expressed themselves adequately with their paper plate props, shift gears and have them use the plates to draw paper-plate faces.

# HUMMER'S ORCHESTRA

Pick a "conductor" who will be the director of the Hummer's Orchestra. When the conductor wishes to increase the volume, he can extend his hands, palms upward. When he desires the volume to be soft, he turns his hands palms down.

When his hands are brought together, the humming is to stop immediately. (You'll find the conductor uses this device quite often in a display of power.)

The conductor can also direct his hummers to go up in pitch or down.

The conducting process is very satisfying to those children who have egomaniacal tendencies—which, you will find, includes most of the class.

By popular demand, you'll have to change conductors often.

# PASS THE FLAG!

Make a little flag out of a stick and construction paper. The object will be to pass the flag from student to student in a limited time, with the flag moving forward only when there is a correct answer.

Correct answer goes forward one; incorrect answer, back one. This is a good device for spelling and math drills.

You, the teacher, can control the game. For example, if there is a low-achieving student who needs confidence, offer him an easier math problem so that his flag will go forward.

The device also works well with parts of speech. "Pass the flag" by naming nouns, adjectives or verbs.

And there are list-making possibilities. "Pass the flag" by naming objects that are usually red (blood, ketchup, etc.) Or "Pass the flag" by listing words associated with Halloween or summer, etc.

It is also good for syllabication: "Pass the flag for two-syllable words.

Or, finally, "Pass the flag" simply for the fun of it—for names of streets in our town or favorite movie stars.

You can get good mileage out of "Passing the flag!"

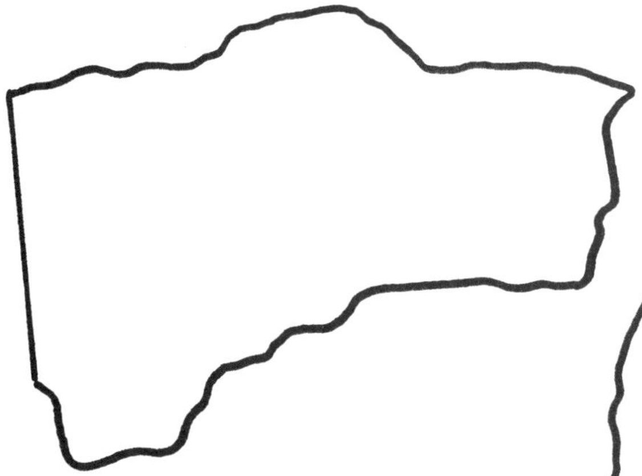
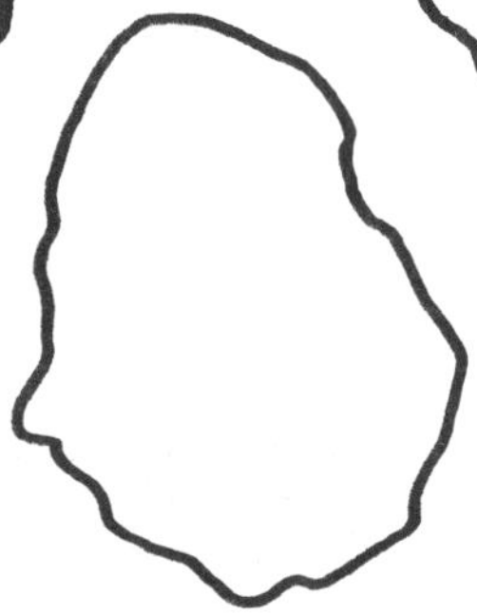

# ART SHAPES

Tear a bunch of shapes out of white or yellow paper so that you have one for each class member. (Tearing is preferable to cutting with scissors because it makes the assignment seem less precious and therefore less inhibiting.)

Give each student a torn shape. With his pencil or crayons he may embellish it in any way he chooses.

It is interesting to note how various children react to this assignment. The truly creative child will make use of the shape in his drawing while a child of lesser ability will merely superimpose a drawing on the shape.

# WRINKLES, ETC.

To set the scene for this discussion session, wrinkle up your face, Mr. Magoo style, and ask:

What makes wrinkles?

Who is the most wrinkled person you know? (Careful, they'll probably say "the teacher.")

Which animals have the most wrinkles? (elephant, turtle, basset hound)

Which animals have hardly any wrinkles at all? (hippopotamus, cat, pig)

Name all the colors found in people's eyes.

What color are dogs' eyes?

What good are fingernails?

What good are eyelashes?

Who has the longest eyelashes in our class?

What do bones do for our bodies? What would we look like without them?

# CONVERSATIONS

Sometimes, it is fun to ramble with ideas. If one of these items doesn't ignite a good discussion, pick another.

Discussion 1: Think about a flagpole. How many ways does it remind you of winter?

Possibilities—A flagpole is shaped like an icicle. Its name—pole—reminds one of the North Pole. Sometimes, flagpoles have a ball on the top, like a snowball or Christmas ornament. A flagpole could be like the trunk of a Christmas tree. A flagpole can get snowed on.

Discussion 2: Think of the blood veins in your body. What man-made things might remind you of the way blood flows through your body?

Possibilities—A highway system with all the cars moving as seen from a plane. Plumbing with water moving. A telephone system. All of these things consist of networks set up to allow something to flow through them.

Discussion 3: Name the different things you find when you turn over a large rock.

Discussion 4: Name the things under your bed right now.

# PICTURE SHORTHAND

These are quick little sketches you can make one at a time on the blackboard. They are abstractions which allow for various points of view.

Most children are adept at decoding visual abstractions such as these and enjoy doing them.

Be sure to allow enough time between drawings to include many possible interpretations, giving children time to explain their thinking.

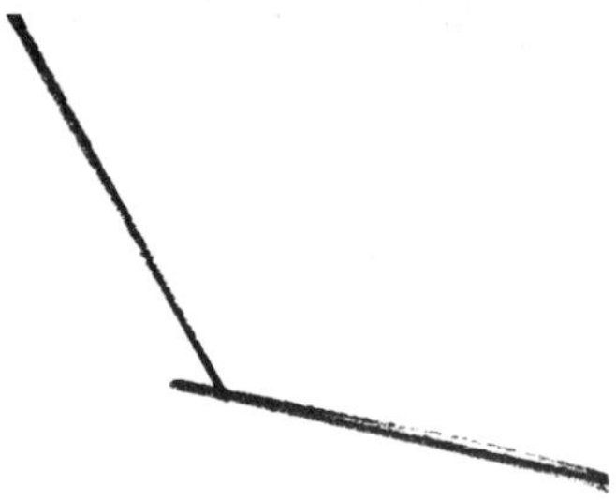

Hands of clock, person sitting

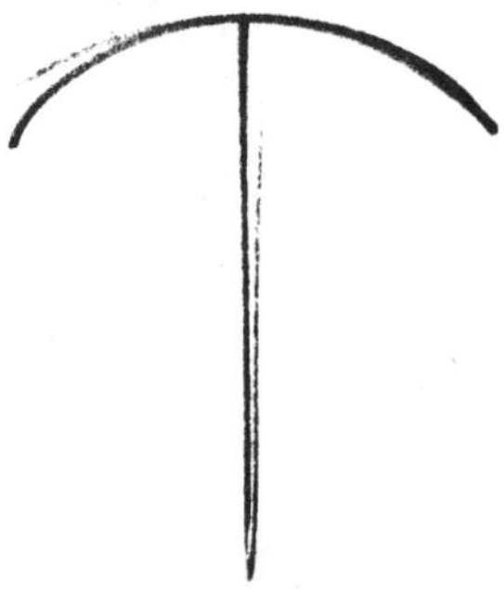

Umbrella

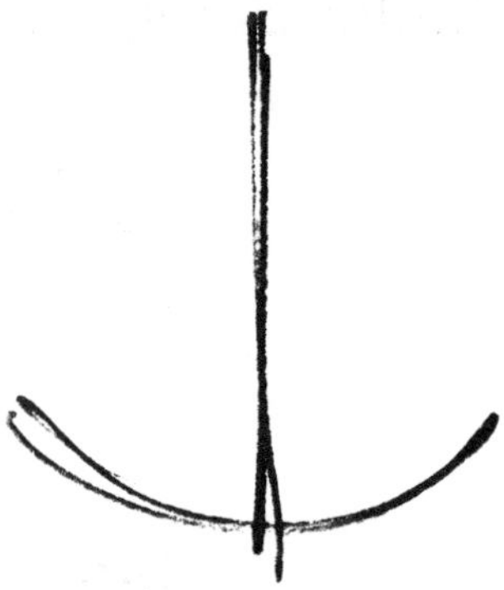

Anchor

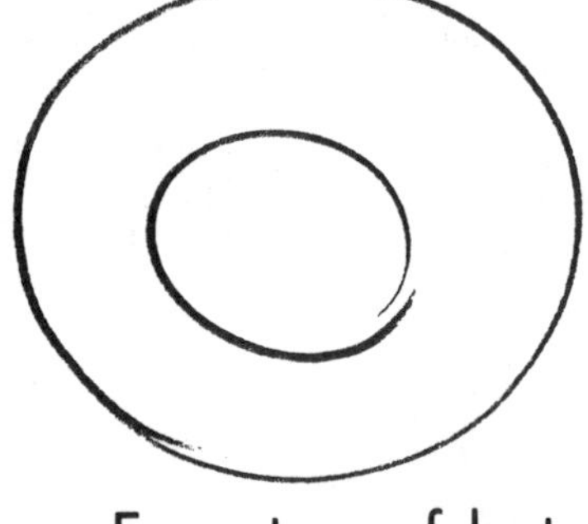

Egg, top of hat, eye, doughnut

Flower, snowflake, bug

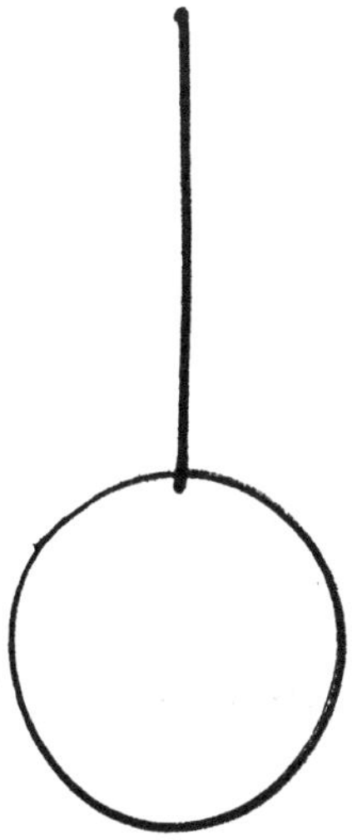

Yo-yo

Lollipop

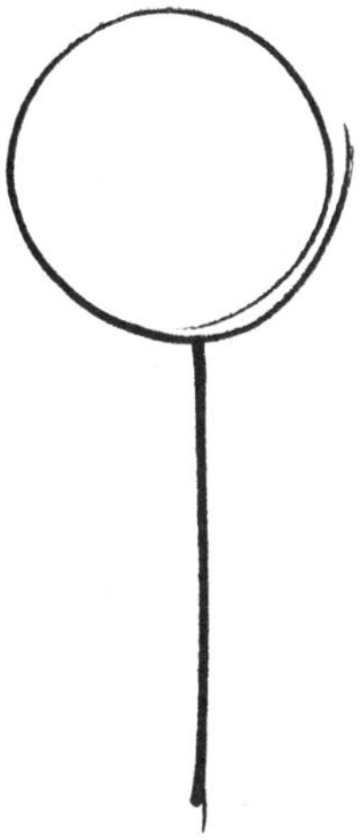

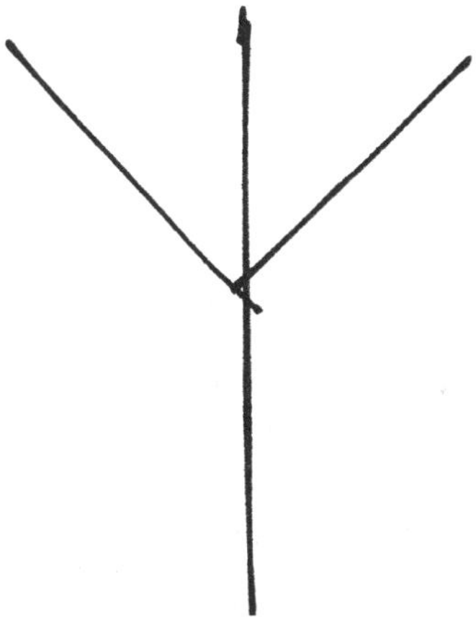

Tree, bird's claw

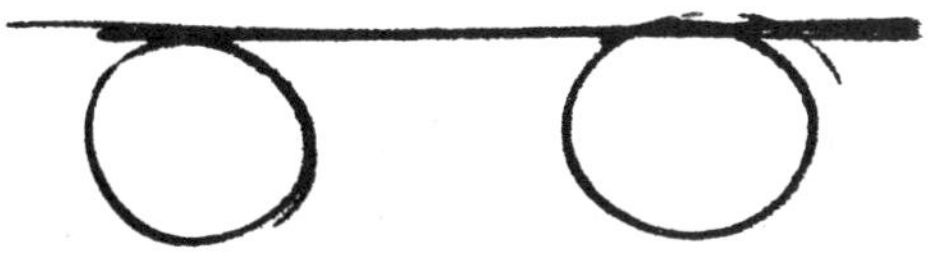

Roller skate, car, truck

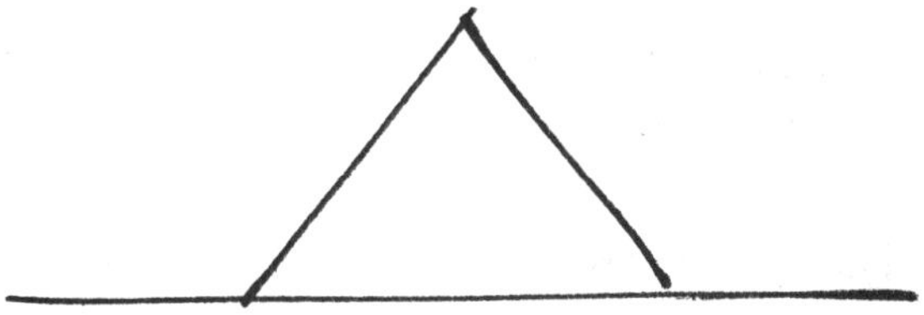

Mountain, roof, hat, sheet of paper falling off the table

Mountain range, saw, teeth

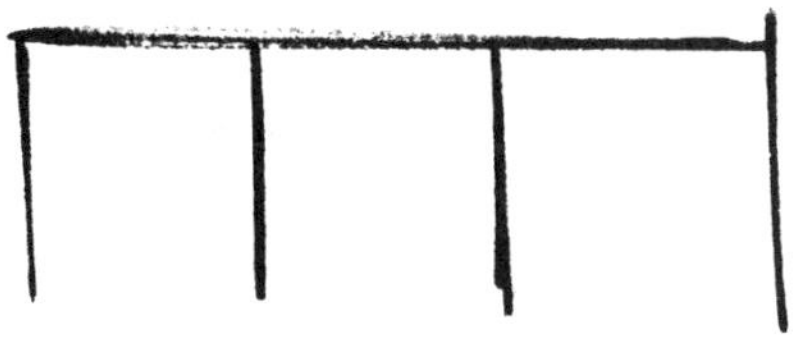

Comb, telephone poles, shingles

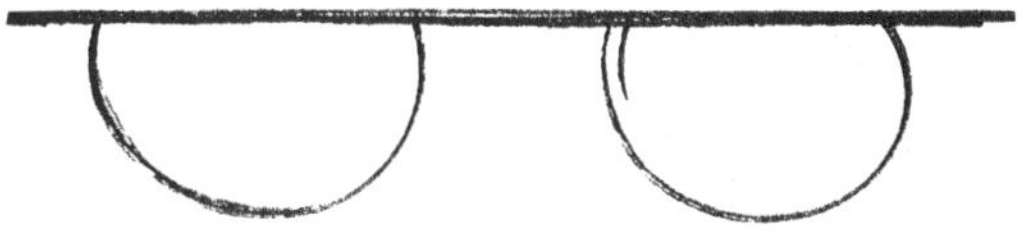

Eyes, drops of water

# BRAINSTORMING

Blackboard brainstorming is invigorating. Put up one word, such as snow. Tell children you want five one-word associations of anything having to do with snow. The action might go like this:

Snow

cold
winter
ice
fun
sleds

Then circle one of the five words and ask for five more associations from the circled word.

swimming
movies
recess
summer
laughing

Circle recess, or whatever, and continue. . .

# OPPOSITE ANTICS

Remove all cards numbered two through ten from the deck. From this stack, count out one card for each child in your class—then take away one card and insert one face card. This means you now have a card for every member of your class. Shuffle.

Pass out one card to each child and tell the students not to let anyone else see what they are holding.

Explain that one child in the class has been given a face card, and that particular person is to do the opposite of what everyone else is instructed to do. (For example, if the class is told to raise right hands, the person with the face card raises his left hand.)

Instructions should be given rapidly so that actions are short in duration, giving the special student a better chance to fool class members.

After children have carried out the instructions, have them guess who they think was "it." The game is easily repeated by collecting cards and re-distributing them.

The instructions are:

1. Raise your right hand.

2. Touch your left ear.

3. Shake your right foot.

4. Smile.

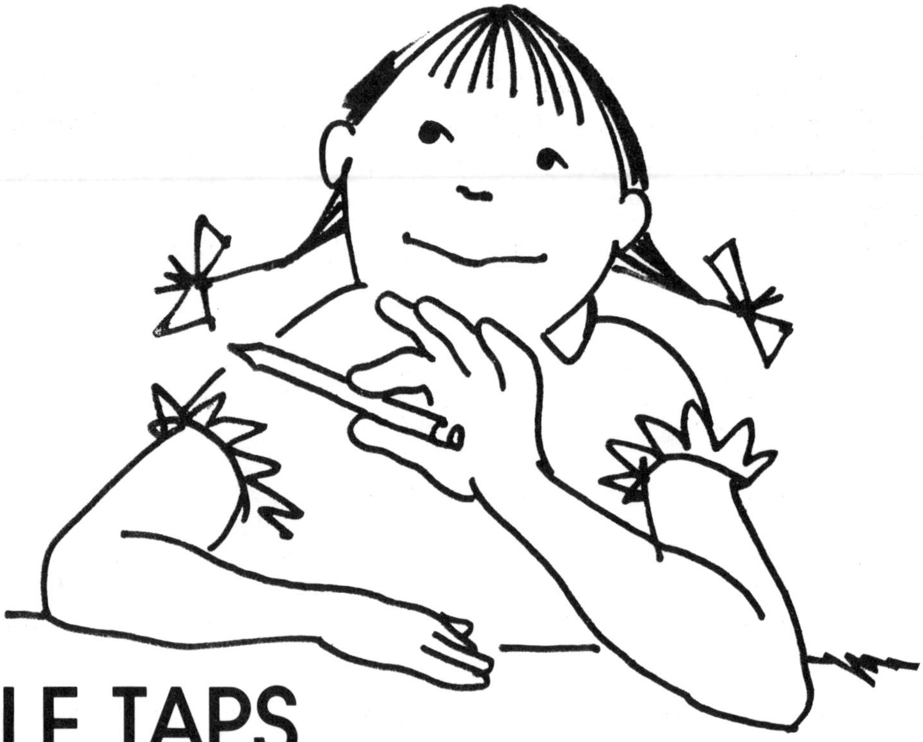

# TABLE TAPS

Have a pencil ready and tell the children they'll need a pencil, also.

Then start tapping a very simple, short rhythm on a table top, which the children can imitate on their desk tops.

The more you play this game, the better you'll get at inventing rhythms. Children will be able to reproduce the rhythms more readily with practice, also.

There are many other ways to tap–by using your knuckles, or the knuckles combined with the flat of your hand. For a different sound, use tips of fingers, or elbows, feet, erasers, rulers.

Let various class members take turns as rhythm leaders sometimes.

This simple activity will be a class favorite—very satisfying after a tough morning of work.

# PAPER NONSENSE

Here are several ideas based on manipulation of a simple piece of paper. Tell the students that they are going to play a game based on following directions, thinking, and having a steady hand.

Each child will need a sheet of 8 1/2 x 11 paper. Ask them to:

1. Tear a strip of paper an inch or so wide from the bottom of your paper. (Demonstrate.) Make a lot of little folds. What does it look like? (An accordian.) Does it make you think of anything else? (A spring, maybe.) Why does it want to bounce back? (Because paper folds act like little springs.)

2. Now tear a piece about four inches square and fold it in half. Fold it in half again. How many times can you fold it? (All members of the class will be able to fold it the same number of times!)

3. Tear off a one-inch piece of paper like this. (Demonstrate.) Moisten it with your tongue and stick it to your nose. How long will it stay?

4. Tear off the tiniest piece of paper you can.

5. How thick is your piece of paper? (Hard to tell, but you could stack up a hundred sheets and measure and then divide by 100 and you'd have a good idea.)

Note: With the exception of Number 5, all of the activities provide concrete experience with one item—the paper—in a variety of ways. This multi-faceted approach is what learning is all about, isn't it?

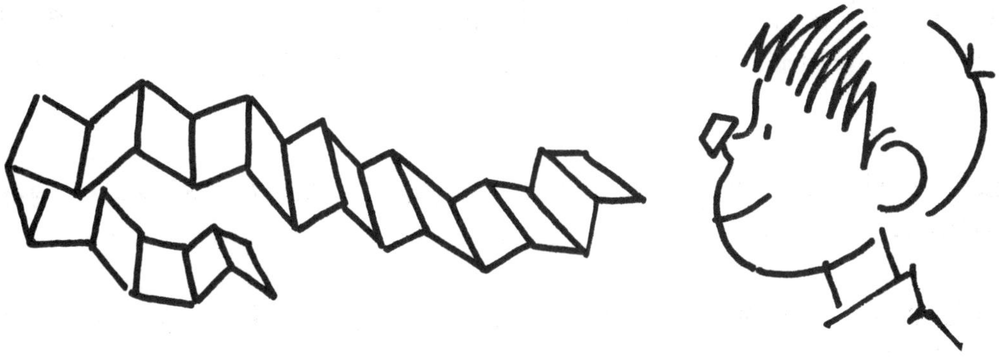

# FINGER PLAYS

Tell your students you are going to give them a number of sentences (actually little story situations) which they are to "act out" using their fingers and hands. Stress that they are to be completely silent during the process. If you see a particularly imaginative response to your instructions, have the child repeat it for the class.

Here are the situations:

1. A little fish swims up to a giant clam, which opens slowly as the fish comes near and, when the fish swims in, closes tightly.

2. A man is being chased by a giant spider!

3. A flower is ready to bloom. First, we see the bud. Then it slowly opens and the flower grows, spreading out its petals in the sun.

4. A little man walks up to a giant and climbs up onto his shoulder. Then he climbs to the top of the giant's head to see what kind of view he will get from there. Just then the giant sneezes and the little man slides down the giant's nose and barely escapes being eaten.

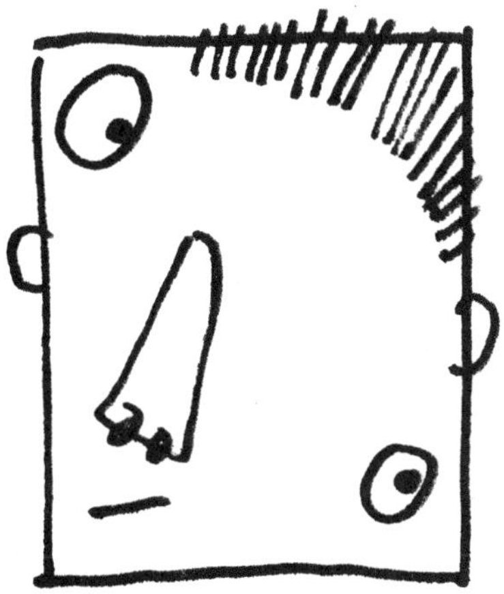

# BLOCKHEADS

Give children 8 1/2 x 11 pieces of paper, tell them to get out a pencil or marker and listen for instructions. Here they are:

1. Draw a large square.
2. Inside the square, draw two circles. (Don't say how big or where.)
3. Draw a line somewhere below the circles.
4. Treat what you have drawn as a face, add some hair and other details, and be ready to share your "person" with the class.

Note: The assignment is interesting because no matter where the two circles and line have been placed, a face can still be made.

Let children compare their drawings. The impreciseness of the directions should made the end products very diverse.

# HUMAN TELEGRAPH

Arrange children in a circle so they can touch hands. Then write a long number on a piece of paper and give it to one of the children. This child then taps each of the digits on the hand of the person standing next to him, who taps it to the next, and so on. The final child serves as the recorder, and is given a piece of paper on which to record the "message."

The object is for the recorder to reproduce the number from the sender as quickly as possible. This means that the first digit must be tapped out and sent along the chain, then the second, and so on, producing a flow of numbers through the chain. Naturally, the numbers will "come out" one at a time at the end of the chain.

For excitement, keep blackboard statistics on "transmission" times and try for a record.

One special note: When the number is tapped, the sender begins with the first digit at the left and works towards the ones column. For a number such as 85231 (don't use zeros), the sender would begin by tapping eight times on his neighbor's hand, then five times and so forth.

# WEATHER WISE

Tell the children that we have many strange sayings in our language that we use all the time. The ones you are going to share are based on weather. Have children comment on what each saying means.

| | |
|---|---|
| It's raining cats and dogs. | (raining hard) |
| She has a sunny disposition. | (always cheery) |
| He runs like the wind. | (fast) |
| I haven't the foggiest idea. | (unclear) |
| Saving for a rainy day. | (putting away money now for the time when you're short of it later.) |
| He stormed out of the house. | (mad) |
| When it rains, it pours. | (when one bad thing happens, other bad things seem to follow) |

# SPARE PARTS

Begin this activity by having the children imitate you as you touch your nose, ears, eyes, feet, elbows, knees, chin, etc. as a way of warming up for what is to follow.

Then say that a lot of inventions help do the work of various parts of our bodies. Tell the students that you'll name some inventions. They are to tell you what part of the body they help.

Telephone—(ear)
Automobile—(legs)
Computer—(brain)
Binoculars—(eyes)
Smoke detector—(nose)
Microphone—(voice and ears)
Typewriter—(hands)
Egg beater—(hands)
Magnifying glass—(eyes)
Escalator—(legs)
Riding lawn mower—(legs)

# CARD CUES

Make a card for every student in the class. On each card, write the following list of words, keeping the words in this order: Sneeze, cough, 3 sneezes, soft laughing, louder laughing, yawn, "Joe!", "Joe!", "Ouch," sneeze, 3 sneezes, chirping, buzzing, soft sneeze.

Explain to the children you are going to tell them a little story and that whenever you pause, they should do whatever is written on the card—following the order in which the words are written.

If chaos results from this activity (with one or two children missing the cues on purpose or doing them inappropriately) have the offenders sit out the rest of the story. They'll shape up, because children want to participate in this activity. You'll find, by popular demand, you'll run through the story two or three times.

> I didn't feel like going to school today. The trouble was, I woke up sneezing. I would (sneeze) and then (cough). What I didn't know was that my brother had tiptoed into my bedroom the night before and sprinkled my room with pepper. That's why I was always making big (3 sneezes). My brother was standing on the other side of the door listening to me. He was trying to keep quiet but couldn't stop (laughing). Then when I heard him (louder laughing), I knew what had happened. I was good and awake by now, although I was still (yawning). I yelled to him, ("Joe!") get in here! I was really mad. Now I could see how the pepper was all over everything. It was even under my bed. I yelled again, ("Joe!") get in here! He came in with a blank expression on his face, like he hadn't done anything, pretending not to notice the pepper all over everything, including the floor. He was being so clever that he accidentally slipped on some of it and fell down. He said ("Ouch!"). "Serves you right," I told him, "now get busy and (sneeze) clean this mess up." I stumbled over to the window to get some fresh air because by now he, too, was (sneezing). From outside, we could hear a robin (chirping) and a bee (buzzing) on a bunch of flowers. Then, the funniest thing happened! I heard the bee (sneeze)! Some practical jokes aren't funny, but the next day I wound string all over Joe's room just to teach him a lesson. Now we're even. And we're friends.

Sometimes my eyes sting. They
get red. Some eyes are blue and
some are green and brown. My
dad has hazel eyes. Cindy, Cindy
Cindy Cindy eyes can wink and
blink. Eyldroppers put drops
in your eyes Cindy Cindy, Cindy
The black in your eye is a pupil

# ASSOCIATIONS

Say to the children: For the next three minutes, write everything you can possibly think of about eyes. Write in cursive. Don't ever stop writing. If you run out of ideas, just write your name over and over until you think of something else.

Note to teacher: Other possible subjects are buttons, frying pans, spoons. These subjects are purposely narrow to make the assignment more interesting. Writing about "summer" would be no fun at all since the subject is frustratingly broad for three minutes. You will be surprised just how many associations there are for a suggested topic, and for some strange reason—if it is not overused—children enjoy silent, sustained writing.

It has educational merits, also—unblocking thinking, letting ideas flow.

# A PAT ON THE BACK!

Give each student a piece of 8 1/2 x 11 paper. Tell the children you are going to give them a number that is very important for them to remember, but they may not write it down. However, the paper can be used in any way they wish to help them remember that important number!

Then give them a number without any zeros, such as 47692.

For the child who discovers he can "code" the number by making a series of little tears on the edges of his paper, a pat on the back!

Put a thumbtack point up on the floor by each child's desk. Tell the children they must pick up the tack and put it on their desk top, but may not touch the tack with their hands. Tell them they may use one "tool" from their desks if they wish.

For the child who discovers the tack may be picked up by sticking the point into a pencil eraser or a regular eraser, a pat on the back!

Give each child a piece of paper and a short length of tape. Tell them they must invent something that will hold a book above the top of their desks.

For the child who rolls a strong cylinder or folds an accordian shape, a pat on the back!

# DODGE THE TEACHER!

This is one of the few elimination games in the book. It has been included simply because guessing games are fun, and out-guessing the teacher is even more fun! The tempo of this activity should be kept very fast, so that "eliminated" students do not have very long to wait for the next game.

First, draw a rectangle on the blackboard roughly the size of the top of a student desk.

Give each child a playing card.

Explain to the class that their desk tops are going to be their playing surface. They are going to play a game which involves placing their card in either the center of their desk or at any of the four corners.

Tell them you have a desk top, too. Yours is drawn on the board and, instead of a card, you will use an "x."

The children are going to try to second-guess where you'll put your "x" by placing their card in one of the five positions and hoping you don't place your "x" in the same position. If you do, they're out and must stand silently until the game is finished.

You should mention that you will not peek in advance at the positioning of the children's cards before you select the position for your "x."

Children still in the game may move their cards to new positions, or leave them in the same place, before you place your next "x."

Always erase your previous "x" before making another.

# A CARD CAPER

Hand out a playing card to each student. Have him place the card on his head. The last child to have the card on his head is the "winner." All of this must be done in an environment of complete concentration—no talking.

Instructions:

1. Clap your hands.
2. Stand up and sit down.
3. Move your head to the right and then the left. Do this three times.
4. Reach down and touch your shoe.
5. Anyone who still has a card on top of his head, walk to the blackboard, touch it and return to your seat.

# ANIMAL ABSTRACTIONS

This activity is adapted from "The Great Unbored Bulletin Board Book." It is used here because it is such an interesting way to spend time while waiting for lunch or at the end of the day.

You will find that children will respond enthusiastically to this series of abstractions. In general, only one clue to the animal's identity is provided. Occasionally, more than one particular answer is correct, as in the case of the animal with the pocket. Most children will see it as a kangaroo, although it could be any marsupial.

Begin this activity by drawing the first five animals quickly on the board. By seeing several at once, children will be able to "get into" the abstraction and will readily see that the circle is the common element of all the animals presented.

After the class has guessed the first five, draw the rest one at a time in order to "savor" the process.

Resist the temptation to help the children too much. Let them play with each challenge before giving them any hints. You will probably not need to help them at all—there are always a few children who will perceive them instantly. For that reason, instruct children not to spoil the guessing process for others by shouting out the answers.

In case you are having a hard time yourself, the answers are: pig, elephant, bat, rhinoceros, kangaroo, beaver, cow, camel, porcupine, cat, rabbit, leopard, skunk, zebra, raccoon.

# CLOTHESLINES

Explain that this is a riddle activity in which all the answers have something to do with what we wear.

1. What does a dog or cat do when he is too hot? (pants)

2. What do you sometimes forget to put back on the toothpaste? (cap)

3. This is the same as something a boxer does. What is it? (sock)

4. Back in your grandmother's day when people wanted to chase away a fly, what did they say? (shoo)

5. Put your fingers together like this: 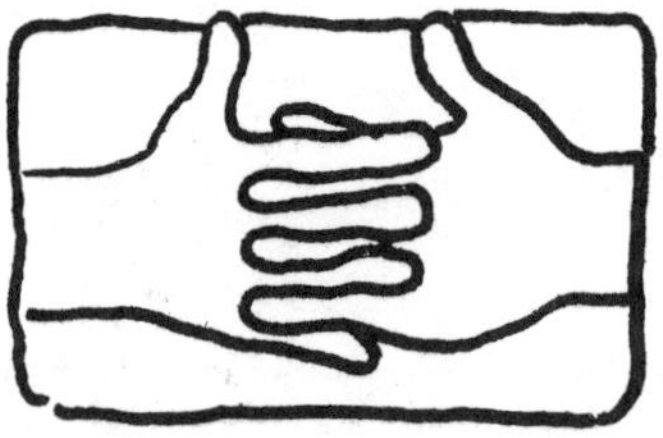

   There's something a lot of you have on as part of your clothes which you should be reminded of. (zipper)

6. What a new layer of paint on your home is called. (coat)

7. What telephones do. (ring)

8. How water gets from your house to your garden. (hose)

# BEAN PUT-ON

One time activity and one time only

A little levity in the classroom doesn't hurt a thing.

Give each student a bean. Tell him to place it on the top of his desk and put a bit of saliva on it for moisture.

Announce that the class will get to go to lunch when the first bean sprouts and then deadpan it.

You will get a lively discussion.

# FOR BIRDBRAINS

Ask the children to close their eyes for a moment and picture various kinds of birds.

Then ask them these questions:

What kind of bird has a name like:

1. Somebody stealing something?
2. Something you do after you chew your food?
3. Something used in building tall buildings or to lift heavy objects?
4. Something that makes a musical sound without opening your mouth?
5. Something that rhymes with an orange vegetable?
6. The color of the sky and a letter that comes before the letter K?
7. Something you do when you don't want to get hit?

(robin)
(swallow)
(crane)
(hummingbird)
(carrot-parrot)
(blue jay)
(duck)

# TEACHER'S LUNCH

The following activity is marvelously simple and the results are tremendous—if you ham it up.

Give children 4-inch squares of paper and tell them to draw one thing you the teacher can eat for lunch. (You might say that you forgot your lunch this day, and they can help.)

Then, take a plate around the room and collect the lunch items. This is where your own brand of creative dramatics comes into play. React to the hilt when you collect the protein gained from the boy who drew you a picture of worms, keep track of the number of pizzas you get.

Later, you may even want to graph the results. . .seven pizzas, eleven tacos, etc.

# LETTER LANGUAGE

Write on the blackboard:

i c u.

i c a b.

g, i 8 a p.

i c y u 8 a p.

a b 8 a p, 2.

i 8 4.

o k.

Have various students read the letters in each "sentence." Do not tell them at first that the letters and numbers make up a story. Then, have one person read the whole thing as a unit.

Afterwards, brainstorm letter-number combinations which sound like real words, like mt for empty, n2 for into, tp for teepee, b4 for before, and qt for cutie.

This activity takes a very short time, so use it on a day when you have just a couple of minutes to kill. It is included because children find the letter reading entertaining.

# THE GREAT PAPER RACE

Tear a strip of paper approximately two by eight inches. Fold it in the middle as shown. Tell students to take out their longest pencils, which will be needed for the paper race.

The object is to pass the paper as quickly as possible around the room. This is accomplished by balancing the paper strip on the pencil and passing it to the next person who is also holding a pencil. No one is allowed actually to touch the paper.

If either the paper or pencil drops, the paper pass begins again.

Variations: Start paper strips from opposite ends of the room and see which one gets to the middle faster.

If you have rows, start paper strips from back to front and see which row wins.

# CLASSIFICATION GAME

Write on the blackboard "Everything soft." Then have children suggest 20 or so soft items you write down. Do not erase.

Next, write the words "Soft and bigger than a globe" and call for answers for items with these two properties.

Finally, write "Soft, bigger than a globe, man-made"—and watch the list get shorter.

The educational by-product of this, of course, is for children to understand that, as more properties are assigned, the harder the challenge.

This is a good "thinking cap" game.

# PLAY-BY-PLAY

Call several students to the front of the room and have them pantomime a sporting activity such as football or baseball.

While the pantomime is going on, other children take turns announcing what they think is happening.

If you want to get fancy, have a play-by-play man and a "color" man as well!

If you have a tape recorder handy, you may want to use it for "instant replays."

Note: This is one activity which requires the services of fluent talkers to be the sports announcers. Certainly, you have one or two!

# FIRST WORD

Have the students sit quietly for a couple of minutes with their heads down on their desks. They are to close their eyes and breathe softly, making no noise. In a very quiet voice, tell them you want them to think about anything they please.

At the end of the time period, instruct them to take out a piece of paper, still being very quiet. When they have done that, break into this introspective atmosphere with a command: They are to write down the first word that pops into their heads NOW.

Let whoever wants to share his word tell about why he wrote what he did.

# A RIDICULOUS ASSIGNMENT

This assignment is ridiculous. That's why children like it. As you know, children love nicknames and word play. What teacher doesn't have a second name she may or may not know about? As Mrs. Rasmussen, I heard my nickname once or twice—Mrs. Raspberry. It could have been worse.

Use this natural impulse to advantage by having children write their own names backwards on a piece of paper.

My name would read aterg nessumsar.

Phonics enters into the picture here, because the child will not only write his name backwards, he must say it.

You go first, then have each child take a turn. It's a sure bet there will be many laughs.

# INDEX

1-800-676-0459

# Other Publications by Tin Man Press

## BOOKS

IS IT FRIDAY ALREADY? LEARNING CENTERS THAT WORK

THE GREAT UNBORED BULLETIN BOARD BOOK I

THE GREAT UNBORED BULLETIN BOARD BOOK II

THE GREAT UNBORED BLACKBOARD BOOK

OPQ, OFFBEAT ADVENTURES WITH THE ALPHABET

NIFTY FIFTY

BRAIN STATIONS

PLAY BY THE RULES

IDEAS TO GO

SMART SNIPS

WAKERUPPERS

T IS FOR THINK

ARE THEY THINKING?

WAITING FOR LUNCH

LOOSEN UP!

## CARD SETS

THE DISCOVER! SERIES

ADVENTURES OF A DOT SERIES

LINEWORK

AN ALPHABET YOU'VE NEVER MET